A Gift For:

_____

From:

_____

Published in Nashville, Tennessee, by Thomas Nelson, Inc.

Unless otherwise indicated, Scripture quotations used in this book are from
The New King James Version® Copyright © 1979, 1980, 1982, 2005 by Thomas Nelson, Inc.

Scripture quotations marked NCV are taken from *The Holy Bible, New Century Version*,
copyright © 1987, 1988, 1991 by Word Publishing, Dallas, Texas, 75039. Used by permission.

Scripture quotations marked NIV from the *Holy Bible, New International Version*®.
Copyright © 1973, 1978, 1984 by International Bible Society.
Used by permission of Zondervan Publishing House. All rights reserved.

Scripture quotations marked NLT are taken from the *Holy Bible, New Living Translation*, copyright © 1996.
Used by permission of Tyndale House Publishers, Inc., Wheaton, Illinois 60189. All rights reserved.

Designed by Greg Jackson, Thinkpen Design, LLC

ISBN 10: 1-59145-550-2
ISBN 13: 978-1-59145-550-9

Printed in the United States of America

A MAN AFTER GOD'S HEART

When a Father's Spirit Soars

THOMAS NELSON PUBLISHERS
Since 1798

TABLE OF CONTENTS

*May our Lord Jesus Christ himself
and God our Father encourage you
and strengthen you in every good thing
you do and say. God loved us,
and through his grace he gave us
a good hope and encouragement
that continues forever.*

2 THESSALONIANS 2:16–17 NCV

REAL MEN ARE COMMITTED

No one ever said being a dad was easy. It takes guts to persevere through the questions and decisions and sacrifices of fatherhood. And yet it's so worth the effort.

Our commitment to our kids often takes us to amazing—and sometimes humorous—places. Sometimes we cry with our kids, sometimes we laugh with them, and sometimes we grit our teeth in frustration. But no matter how much time and energy we sacrifice on behalf of our kids, we always get it back when we hear, "I love you, Daddy."

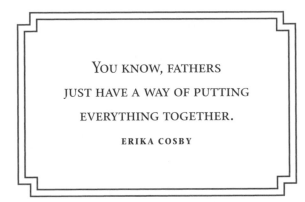

YOU KNOW, FATHERS
JUST HAVE A WAY OF PUTTING
EVERYTHING TOGETHER.

ERIKA COSBY

FREE WALKER

GLENN A. HASCALL

My afternoon ritual was about to be spoiled. I had picked up my children from school and advised them of the value of personally attending to their homework as I sat back down to my computer to work.

"Dad?" my daughter, Alyssa, called from the hall, heading straight for my room.

"Yeah?" I muttered as I tried to get my fingers to type a creative sentence on building a successful online business—and failed at the task.

"I'm chief zoologist in class this week and I have to feed some sort of genetic cross between a mouse and a rat. They're so cute! Then there's this black and yellow salamander that makes your hands numb if you touch him. Anyway, he eats crickets, and since I hear one outside my window every night, I bet I could find one to take to school. I don't know how much he eats, but I'm pretty sure it's at least one every day. Do you think he eats the legs too? That would be kind of disgusting, but I wouldn't mind watching, just once. Anyway, if it's okay with you, I'd like to go outside and try to catch a couple of crickets for school. Of course, I would probably need a jar. What do you think, Dad? . . . Dad? . . . *Dad*!"

The only thing my mind could conceive in that moment was some sort of strange online company that provides crickets to schools. Suddenly I remember my daughter had been speaking. "I'm sorry, Alyssa, did you say something?"

"She wants to go catch crickets," my seven-year-old son, Ryan, said with an amused smile.

"Oh, sure, go right ahead," I said as I tried to makes sense of affiliate programs and shopping carts.

Not five minutes later, I heard my daughter squeal, "Ewww!" then heard my son's voice from the top of the stairs. "Hey, Dad, could you come and kill some spiders?"

"I thought you were going to find some crickets," I called somewhat absently.

"We were, but there's a big spider in the window well and we can't get the cricket," Ryan replied.

Being somewhat willing to give my brain a rest from the world of online marketing, I ventured out to the shed to retrieve a rake. The debris that had gathered in the window well was removed and a large spider scrambled out. It was an easy decision to send it on to its eternal reward. "There, all taken care of," I said, pleased with the ease with which this crisis was managed.

"Eww, Dad! There's more down there." Alyssa pointed and threw in a few squeals for effect.

I summarily sent fifteen additional spiders to the great web in the sky and, once again, thought my fatherly duties were over for this particular calamity.

"While you're down there, do you want to find the cricket, Dad? I'd be too afraid of the spiders," Alyssa asked as she handed an empty water bottle my direction.

Four crickets and a large beetle later, I exhumed myself from the hole and watched the crickets chirping in their plastic cages. My daughter peppered me with questions about whether the cricket felt any pain when being munched on by an amphibian. Some questions have no good answer.

As my wife and I prayed with our children that night, my son looked at me and began to tear up. "Dad, do you think it will hurt when Walker gets eaten tomorrow?"

"Walker? Who's that, son?" I asked.

"The beetle you caught today. I don't want him to get eaten, Dad." My seven-year-old was on the verge of sobs, the racking variety.

I had no idea he had named the beast. That's never a good sign. "I'll tell you what, Ryan. I will move Walker to another bottle and you can let him go tomorrow."

"He has a family, you know."

"He does?"

"They'll miss him. Everyone needs a dad."

For the first time that day, my mind was clear, undistracted. My son's tears had stirred me. Walker must be freed tonight, I decided.

It was dark out when Ryan took Walker back to the window well, and the symbolism of a beetle running home to his family taught this daddy a valuable lesson: No matter what other responsibilities we have, there will always be someone needing Dad and waiting for him to show up. And those someones are more important than anything the world has to offer.

Thanks for the reminder, Walker. May your tribe increase—next door. ◆

Let us not become weary in doing good, for at the proper time we will reap a harvest if we do not give up.

GALATIANS 6:9 NIV

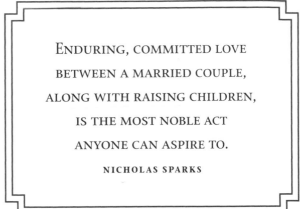

ENDURING, COMMITTED LOVE
BETWEEN A MARRIED COUPLE,
ALONG WITH RAISING CHILDREN,
IS THE MOST NOBLE ACT
ANYONE CAN ASPIRE TO.

NICHOLAS SPARKS

Love never ends.

1 CORINTHIANS 13:8A NCV

A Big Job

Signing up for fatherhood means signing up for the long haul. Eighteen years of parenting amounts to approximately:

- 6,000 diaper changes—per kid
- 4,100 bedtimes
- 400 nights spent waiting for kids to come home from dates (depending on how many kids you have and how old they are when they start dating)
- Anywhere between $8,490 and $12,810 spent on clothes (depending on how many of your children are girls).

Then there are other dad duties that are harder to quantify, of course: horsey rides, soccer games, oil changes, and the like. But there are also innumerable kisses and hugs, toddler jokes and dances, and trips to the park. Even with all the responsibility they bring, the eighteen years we spend fathering our children are the shortest—and most incredible—years of our lives. ◆

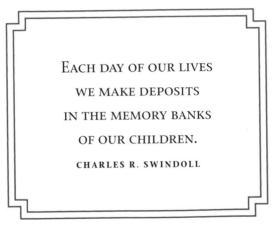

EACH DAY OF OUR LIVES
WE MAKE DEPOSITS
IN THE MEMORY BANKS
OF OUR CHILDREN.

CHARLES R. SWINDOLL

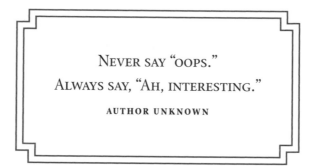

NEVER SAY "OOPS."

ALWAYS SAY, "AH, INTERESTING."

AUTHOR UNKNOWN

Tuxedo Swimming

MICHAEL T. POWERS

Recently I took my three-year-old, Caleb, to his first swimming lessons at the local YMCA. I had been looking forward to some father-son bonding time ever since my wife had suggested swimming lessons earlier in the year. The day before our first class, zoned out after working the night shift, I asked my wife, Kristi, if she could call the YMCA to find out what we were supposed to bring, what time we were to be there, and any other important details. I wanted to make sure I knew what I was getting into.

We left half an hour early, just to make sure we were there on time, and went to the locker room to change. We got our swimsuits on, put the rest of our clothes in a gym bag, and proceeded to make our way out through the showers and into the pool area. I was really looking forward to this. Me, my boy, our swimsuits, and a pool full of water—what could be better?

Well, I rounded the corner, holding hands with my excited son, and an inaudible gasp of horror escaped me. There in the hall next to the pool were ten to fifteen parents and their young children. All the children had their swimsuits on, but every single one of the parents was fully dressed. Let me rephrase that: All the mothers were fully dressed. There was not another father to be seen for miles. I was the only guy. Some mothers were in dresses and power suits as if they had just come from the office, while others wore jeans and T-shirts—but all of them had actual clothes on.

I could just hear what they were thinking:

"Who's the three-year-old with hair on his chest?"

"Can a man really have a chest that goes into his body instead of out?"

"I thought you had to be a corpse to have skin that white."

"I wonder if he has some kind of parasite. Something has to be stealing his nourishment."

I wanted to scream back at them: "I tried lifting weights, but they're too heavy!"

One of the nice high school girls who were teaching the swim class started explaining that the parents were to stay out in the hall and watch their kids through the large windows, only to come near the pool if their children were crying or misbehaving, so that the kids wouldn't be distracted while they were taught not to drown.

As she spoke, I slowly reached into my gym bag and pulled out my T-shirt. Trying my best to be cool and nonchalant, I slipped the cottony covering over the top half of my body, and by the time she was done talking I was fully clothed and decidedly less conspicuous.

Caleb had a great time as I watched through the windows and tried to avoid any possible conversation with another human being.

When I came home, the first thing out of Kristi's mouth was, "How come you're not wet?"

After I explained what had transpired, she laughed and laughed until her stomach hurt. For some reason, even after the phone call, we were both under the impression that I would get to frolic in the water too. The best part of the whole story is: I have to go back and face these people again today at 4:30, and twice a week for the next month or so.

I think I might rent a tux for today's swimming lesson. ◆

A happy heart is like good medicine.

PROVERBS 17:22A NCV

Perseverance

The Bible is full of examples of men who followed through and were rewarded for it—

- Caleb explored the Promised Land with bravery and persistence, trusting in the promise of the Lord when everyone else was too afraid to continue. Because of his dedication, God promised that his descendents would enter the Promised Land (Numbers 14:24).

- The apostle Paul made it his life's work to encourage and strengthen the Church, persevering through beatings, imprisonment, a shipwreck that left him stranded in the open sea for a night and a day, sleep deprivation, and attacks of criticism from his own flock (2 Corinthians 11:22–33). Yet he experienced an inner strength and peace that enabled him to further the Gospel like no one else.

- Jesus stated plainly, "My food is to do the will of Him who sent Me, and to finish His work" (John 4:34). To do

God's will, Jesus endured public ridicule, long days of travel—and death on a cross. Because of this, "God also has highly exalted Him and given Him the name which is above every name" (Philippians 2:9).

All of these men committed to causes that were greater than themselves; they took on missions from God and determined to do His will above all else. And one of the highest callings God bestows is the honor of raising children.

As you commit to be there for your kids, remember that God rewards perseverance and obedience. Under His care, your efforts will pay off, and you and your children will thrive. ◆

Delight yourself also in the LORD,
And He shall give you the desires of your heart.
Commit your way to the LORD,
Trust also in Him, And He shall bring it to pass.

PSALM 37:4–5

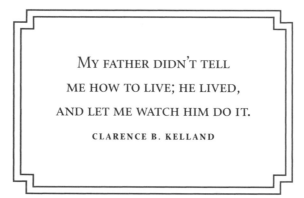

MY FATHER DIDN'T TELL
ME HOW TO LIVE; HE LIVED,
AND LET ME WATCH HIM DO IT.

CLARENCE B. KELLAND

WHERE THERE'S A WILL, THERE'S A WAY

RENIE BURGHARDT

Before World War II, we were a prosperous family. My Apa (Hungarian for "grandfather") was the only father I knew and served as a judge in the small Hungarian town where we lived. Apa and Anya (my grandmother) also owned a farm where I often watched Apa till the soil with the help of his two oxen. He never shrank from hard work, and he took great pride in providing for his family.

And then the war came and everything was gone, just like a cloud of smoke.

When the war ended, life did not improve for the people of Hungary. Soviet occupation and the new communist government brought with it new atrocities and hardships. Because Apa spoke out against these atrocities, he was soon in danger of being imprisoned. We fled to freedom in the late fall of 1947.

A refugee camp in Austria became our new home. Called a displaced persons camp, Camp Spittal housed hundreds of destitute refugees. Although the camp was dismal and cramped, we were grateful to God to be there, for we had a roof over our heads, were clothed with donated goods, and were fed daily. So what did it matter that we didn't have a penny to our name?

However, it mattered a great deal to Apa. He hated living off the charity of others, hated not being able to buy me the book I had glanced at longingly when we passed a bookstore in town.

Just beyond our dismal camp home was another world—a beautiful, natural world of mountains, clear, cold streams, rolling hills carpeted with flowers, and small farms dotted with grazing animals. It was this other world that ignited my imagination with its beauty and gave my heart hope. So I often slipped away from the crowded world of the camp and roamed the hills and valleys. On one of these rambles, I soon discovered the beautiful River Drau, just a half-mile walk from the camp. It became my favorite retreat, and one day I told Apa about it.

"A river?" he asked with great interest. "How far is this river from camp?"

"I'm not sure, but it takes me half an hour to walk to it," I replied.

"Good. Tomorrow I'll go to the river with you."

"Oh, Apa, you will love it," said enthusiastically. "It's the Drau River, and it's so beautiful!"

"I have always loved rivers. Rivers benefit people and animals," he replied thoughtfully. I could see ideas clambering across his face.

The following morning, Apa and I set out on our walk to the Drau. Once we were there, I splashed around in the shallow, clear, rushing water while he walked up and down the bank. After a while, I noticed that Apa was cutting some branches from the river willows growing all along the bank. By the time we headed back to camp, he had a large armful of them.

"What are you going to do with them?" I asked as we made our way back to the camp.

"Weave some baskets," Apa replied. I remembered that in the past, Apa's hobby had been weaving. He had made a beautiful settee for Anya and an adorable table and chair for me when I was five. But in the course of the war, all that had been forgotten.

"And what will you do with the baskets?" My curiosity was aroused.

"I will try and sell them to the Austrians."

Soon, Apa found some old boards and bricks and set up a worktable in front of our barrack. Then after peeling the willow branches, he began weaving his first basket. A large crowd soon gathered around to watch him. Some boys volunteered to get more willow branches for him.

"Thank you," Apa told them. "And when I sell my baskets, I will pay you for your help."

Within a short time, there were six beautifully woven baskets ready for market. Apa hung them on a long stick, flung them over his shoulder, and off he went into town, looking something like a hobo peddler, much to Anya's embarrassment. He returned a few hours later with the hobo stick minus the baskets. He had sold every last one. Then he reached into his pocket and pulled something out, handing it to me. It was the new storybook I had been eyeing.

"Oh, thank you, Apa!" I shrieked as I threw my arms around him. "I can't believe you were able to buy it."

"You are very welcome. And never forget—where there is a will, there is always a way."

My dear Apa was a wonderful gift giver. He gave me the book I'd had my heart set on—along with a lesson for life about making the best of the worst situations. I carry his love, determination, and faithfulness with me wherever I go. ◆

Ask, and it will be given to you;
seek, and you will find;
knock, and it will be opened to you.

MATTHEW 7:7

God's Promises for Committed Dads

For God is not unjust to forget your work and labor of love which you have shown toward His name, in that you have ministered to the saints, and do minister.

HEBREWS 6:10

Train up a child in the way he should go,
And when he is old he will not depart from it.

PROVERBS 22:6

Therefore, my beloved brethren, be steadfast,
immovable, always abounding in the work of the Lord,
knowing that your labor is not in vain in the Lord.

1 CORINTHIANS 15:58

Those who refresh others will themselves be refreshed.

PROVERBS 11:25B NLT

When your endurance is fully developed,
you will be perfect and complete, needing nothing.

JAMES 1:4B NLT

*You have filled my heart
with greater joy than when
their grain and new wine abound.*

PSALM 4:7 NIV

REAL MEN CRY SOMETIMES

It's a moment we never forget: The moment we found out we were about to have kids of our own. The only word for it is *joy*—an inexpressible, irrepressible flood of happiness, thankfulness, and pride which often takes the form of tears. And yes, we've cried a few more tears as our careers in fatherhood have continued. Weddings, the first day of kindergarten, the thrill of victory and the agony of defeat—a dad who cares deeply about his kids can't help but feel strongly about the events of daddyhood.

It only makes sense to get a little misty-eyed over fatherhood. Being a father is one of the most incredible experiences there is. ◆

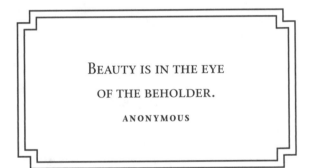

BEAUTY IS IN THE EYE
OF THE BEHOLDER.

ANONYMOUS

THE NEW FATHER FOG

MICHAEL T. POWERS

When my wife, Kristi, found out she was pregnant with our first son, Caleb, she decided to tell me in a creative way. She took me to a nice restaurant for dinner. At the end of our delicious meal, the waitress handed me the check, along with a sealed envelope, which she told me was from someone in the restaurant. I looked around, searching for a familiar face, but found none. I opened it and read the typed message, and as I did, all the employees, including the hostess and the entire kitchen staff, started moving closer to our table.

The message read: "Michael, this is to inform you that you will be changing the kitty litter for the next nine months. In other words, congratulations: You are going to be a father!"

I looked across the table at my beloved wife with disbelief on my face. Within a second, I was bawling like a baby. I had wanted to have children all seven years of our marriage, but Kristi had wanted to wait. This was not something we had planned, and I wasn't emotionally ready for it. There I sat, tears streaming down my face, surrounded by my now crying wife, a gaggle of sobbing waitresses, and a couple of chefs who strode back to the kitchen in a suspicious hurry.

The next eight months were filled with anticipation and moments of wonder. I remember hearing the sound of my baby's heartbeat in the doctor's office. Nothing prepares a man for the moment he hears his child's heartbeat for the first time. It was nothing like I expected—in place of a gentle *thump-thump*, the chugging that came through the speakers sounded just like a train. I realize that most people aren't exactly enthralled by the sound of railway cars, but to me that sound was pure magic.

I remember watching my wife's tummy grow, longing for the day when I would be able to feel Caleb moving inside of her. We would sit for long periods of time, my hands pressed gently against her abdomen, waiting for Caleb to move, but he wouldn't. I would pray that God would give him the hiccups just so I could feel my son through the thin layer that protected him from the outside world.

And then one day, miraculously, he moved, and I connected with my baby for the first time. I waited breathlessly for him to move again, not believing that it had actually happened. I can't even imagine what it must have felt like for Kristi to sense her offspring moving within her.

As I waited for the day of his birth, I would have dreams of seeing him for the first time, intensely vivid dreams of a baby's face that would stay with me long after sleep ended.

Looking back now, I am amazed at how long—and how short—nine months can be. We never did get to rush off to the hospital like so many people do on TV because Caleb decided he liked it too much inside the womb. After three weeks past Kristi's due date, the doctors decided to induce labor. So there we sat in the hospital waiting for something to happen.

Labor finally set in—twenty hours of it. And in the end, Caleb's head was too big for the birth canal, and the doctor told us he would have to do a C-section. At this point I was a little worried, but I trusted that God and the doctors knew what they were doing.

And then it finally happened. I was sitting at the head of the operating table holding Kristi's hand when the doctor said, "Okay, we have a healthy baby boy." Throughout surgery, I'd been afraid to stand up to see what was going on—I figured the doctors and nurses would yell at me and say, "Boy, what do you think you're doing? You sit back down now!" But when I heard the doctor say that he could see the baby, I didn't care if they threw a scalpel at me; I was going to look at my child.

There he was. I could almost hear the angels singing as my precious baby boy entered the world. He was perfect in every way, and the tears began to fall.

"Oh, Kristi! He's beautiful!" was all I could stammer. I was in the "new father fog."

I must have been, because in reality, Caleb looked terrible. His skin color changed about four times in the first five minutes, and he probably could have made the cover of *The National Enquirer*: "Reptile Boy Born in Wisconsin!" His hands and feet were extremely wrinkled, like he had been in the pool too long, and all kinds of bodily secretions were oozing from his pores.

And he also had two heads.

It was the first thing Kristi noticed when the nurse handed Caleb to her for the first time. Because Caleb had gone through twenty hours of labor with his head stuck in the birth canal, it had swollen up like a balloon in two different places, and it really did look like he had two heads. Kristi told me later that she was thoroughly convinced that she had married someone with severe vision problems or a major mental disorder—"My husband called this thing beautiful?"

Being the proud father that I was, however, I figured the extra space in his cranium was simply God's way of helping Caleb store all the brain matter he'd inherited from me. The swelling did go down in a few days, but Caleb wasn't exactly looking his best for the first few weeks.

Nonetheless, I kept telling everyone how beautiful he was. It wasn't until a year or so later, after looking at the video of the birth, that I realized Caleb had looked like a swollen two-headed lizard that had been in the water for too long. To me, he was—and is—the most beautiful creation that had ever appeared on the earth.

I guess fatherhood blinds you to certain things, and you know what they say: Ignorance is bliss. ◆

I thank my God upon every remembrance of you.

PHILIPPIANS 1:3

COUNT YOUR BLESSINGS

What do you like most about being a father? What do you like most about each of your kids? Take a minute to count your blessings and write down the ways being a father has enriched your life. When you're done, pray a prayer of gratitude—and then find a special way to communicate to your kids, "I'm glad I'm your dad." ◆

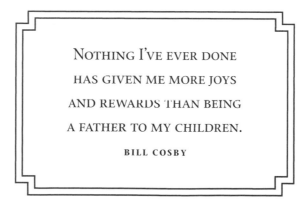

NOTHING I'VE EVER DONE
HAS GIVEN ME MORE JOYS
AND REWARDS THAN BEING
A FATHER TO MY CHILDREN.

BILL COSBY

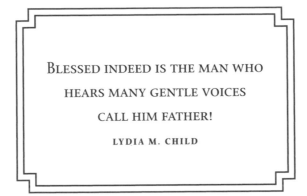

BLESSED INDEED IS THE MAN WHO
HEARS MANY GENTLE VOICES
CALL HIM FATHER!

LYDIA M. CHILD

A VERY LUCKY MAN

ROY C. GIBBS AS TOLD TO NANCY B. GIBBS

Twenty-seven years ago, I stood before a judge and adopted my twin sons, Chad and Brad. Their mom and I had met, fallen in love, and married in a matter of months, and two months later, the boys' biological father gave me the greatest gift I could have ever received. After a six-month waiting period, I legally became the father of two precious little boys.

"You're a very lucky man," the judge announced over us as we stood before the bench. At that moment, we began our life together as a real family. I realized then that I hadn't just married the love of my life; I was joined by the heart with her sons, as well. Our daughter, Becky, was born a couple of years later, and what a joy she brought to our entire family. I never knew a family could be so close. The judge was right. I am a very fortunate man.

The years went on. The kids and I laughed as we played together in the front yard. I coached the boys' midget football team. Since I am a minister of the gospel, I had the privilege of baptizing all three of my children after they made decisions for Christ, becoming not only their father, but also their brother in Christ. What a wonderful opportunity God had given to me. Sometimes I forget that I adopted the boys. We have so much in common that I couldn't imagine a time that we weren't a big happy family.

Before long, the children became teenagers. As they grew older, thankfully, our family grew closer. I tried to put a firm foundation under their feet. And when the time came for the boys to leave for college, I reluctantly gave them their wings to fly. But I still rejoiced every time they came home for a visit and knew that time and distance would never keep us apart.

After they graduated from college, I again found myself standing before a crowd of people in a church with my son, Chad. As his minister, I conducted his wedding ceremony. Brad stood by his side as his best man, while Becky stood nearby as a bridesmaid. Again, I remembered the words the judge had shared with me a quarter of a century earlier: "You are a very lucky man."

When Chad's beautiful bride, Lucy, joined us, I could barely contain my emotions. I had adopted my son, baptized him, and was also given the opportunity to conduct his wedding ceremony. In addition, we were welcoming a new member to our family—I had a beautiful daughter-in-law.

But about a year and a half later, our family encountered a crisis: I faced a major illness for the first time in my life. My son Brad was engaged at the time. I had planned to conduct his wedding as well, but a couple of months before Brad's wedding date, I was scheduled to have open-heart surgery.

Fortunately, with God's blessings, I was well enough to conduct Brad's ceremony. I joined Brad and his beautiful bride, Amy, together as husband and wife. Chad stood beside Brad as his best man, and again Becky stood nearby as a bridesmaid. I realized again—especially in light of my recent health crisis—how blessed I was as I stood before all my children.

Being a family is much more than simply sharing a name. To be a family means to stand together, support each other, and be there for each other through all the good times and bad times in life—baptisms, weddings, anniversaries, funerals.

During my lifetime, God has given me many special gifts, but my most prized are my two sons and beautiful daughter to love forever. Today, as I reflect upon my sons' becoming grooms, I anticipate the time when my daughter, Becky, will become a bride. She will stand before me as I officiate her wedding and we welcome a new son to our family as well.

The judge was right the day that he signed the adoption papers many years earlier, making me the father of two sons. I am a very lucky man to have been afforded so many wonderful opportunities as a father and a minister. I thank God every day for the blessings of my family and home. Yes, Judge, I am a very lucky man. ◆

You have given me
greater joy than those
who have abundant harvests
of grain and wine.

PSALM 4:7 NLT

LOVE IS BLIND

MICHAEL T. POWERS

Recently my wife told me that when she passed by my son's room, she heard him singing about me. Warm fuzzies began tickling my tummy as I thought about my boy singing about his daddy. I really swelled with pride when she told me that his song was comprised of a singsong repetition of "I love my daddy . . . I love my daddy." The bridge of his little tune, however, was "But I don't know why! No, I don't know why!" Then he reprised with "I love my daddy."

Hey, I'll take all the love this little guy has to give me, even if he doesn't know why. ◆

ONE DOES NOT
LOVE ONE'S CHILDREN
JUST BECAUSE THEY ARE
ONE'S CHILDREN
BUT BECAUSE
OF THE FRIENDSHIP
FORMED WHILE
RAISING THEM.

GABRIEL GARCIA MÁRQUEZ

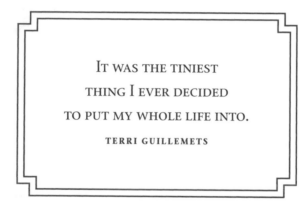

IT WAS THE TINIEST
THING I EVER DECIDED
TO PUT MY WHOLE LIFE INTO.

TERRI GUILLEMETS

Tears of Joy

JEFF ADAMS

After fourteen years of waiting, I held my newborn daughter.

We sat alone in her hospital room. I couldn't stop staring at this latest miracle in my life. Her eyes seemed fixed on me, and I returned her gaze of wonder. All the anguish of the preceding, uncertain months drowned in her big brown eyes. More than once I wiped tears from my cheeks. In a somewhat shaky whisper, I sang "Jesus Loves Me" to my baby daughter.

My wife, Rosemary, and I never imagined adoption would be so difficult. We'd searched from coast to coast and even overseas for a child who would call us Momma and Dada. After more than two dozen failed attempts, we'd all but given up hope.

Then one phone call brightened our outlook. A friend of ours, Brandy, called and said someone had asked her if she knew anyone who wanted to adopt a baby. She did indeed—as our travel agent, Brandy had made arrangements numerous times for us to travel to meet prospective birthparents. When we returned empty-handed, she was devastated along with us, as were our families and other friends. Rosemary described each loss as a miscarriage in her heart, while my own heart grew calloused.

But then the sun broke through the clouds, and soon the best day of our lives arrived—the day Meaghan was born. An 8:00 A.M. drive to the hospital. Labor induced. Waiting. More waiting. No changes. We had lunch at a nearby restaurant, only to receive a page that labor pains had started. We scrambled back to the hospital, and after a few chaotic hours, we finally heard a tiny baby's cry. It was time to welcome Meaghan into our world.

That first night, as I rocked her in my arms, the anguish of the past slipped away. I thought of Jacob who waited fourteen years for his beloved Rachel. I remembered that to him the years seemed like days. Finally, the grief of childless Father's Days would cease.

Then a gentle knock on the almost-closed door threatened our peace, the hallway lights casting a shadow of doubt across our future.

The birth mother had said she didn't want to see Meaghan, and yet here she was in our hospital room. It made me nervous. "Could I hold her?" she asked.

In seconds, a whirlwind of emotions engulfed my heart—fear that she had changed her mind, anger that she would even consider doing so knowing what we'd been through. Numb, I stood up and placed my daughter in her arms.

After she left, I wept in relief. But the relinquishment of her parental rights was more than forty-eight hours away. And months would pass before the court would finalize the adoption. I knew anything could happen, but for right now I could hold my baby.

Two days later, my wife and others witnessed a shaky signature on a legal document that severed all rights of one mother and transplanted them to another. It was then that Hannah told Rosemary the truth about why she returned to the hospital that night: She had been having second thoughts. But that night, "When I heard Jeff singing to Meaghan and then saw him rocking her, I knew I'd made the right decision," she told us.

When Rosemary related the events of two days past, I cried again. The first time, I'd shed tears of fear and relief; now came streams of joy.

Months later, our joy overflowed. At the courthouse, the judge presiding over the legality of Meaghan becoming our daughter seemed perplexed. Thinking he'd discovered a clerical error on the document that would seal the adoption, he asked about her names—the one on the birth certificate and the one she would bear, ours. Both names were identical: Meaghan Elizabeth Adams. "Is this right?" he asked.

"Yes," I said. "That's always been her name."

Hannah knew the name we'd chosen long before the baby was born. She gave our daughter that name, even our last name, rather than her own, meaning that our adoption wouldn't require a name change the way many adoptions do. Meaghan has always been who she will always be.

That day Meaghan became ours officially, legally, although I believe she'd been ours since before she was born. The contentment and joy, the deep sense of security I experienced that day has grown richer and deeper as Meaghan has grown. The joy of being a father overtook me when she was born, and it has never let me go. ◆

*Behold what manner of love
the Father has bestowed
on us, that we should be
called children of God!*

1 JOHN 3:1

GOD'S PROMISES FOR CELEBRATING FATHERHOOD

Behold, children are a heritage from the LORD,
The fruit of the womb is a reward.

PSALM 127:3

Whoever receives one little child
like this in My name receives Me.

MATTHEW 18:5

The father of a good child is very happy;
parents who have wise children
are glad because of them.

PROVERBS 23:24 NCV

The children of Your servants will continue,
And their descendants will be established before You.

PSALM 102:28

The joy of the LORD is your strength.

NEHEMIAH 8:10B

Be strong and courageous.
Do not be afraid or terrified
because of them, for the Lord
your God goes with you; he will
never leave you nor forsake you.

DEUTERONOMY 31:6 NIV

REAL MEN ARE TOUGH

There are times when being a father requires toughness—when we encounter a discipline standoff . . . when someone or something is causing our child problems or pain . . . when it's time to model hard work and dedication.

Sometimes it's hard to take a hard line; sometimes we struggle to determine when to get tough. But there is value in loving, godly toughness—the kind of toughness that gives kids a sense of safety teaches them how to relate to their Heavenly Father. A wise dad is a dad who occasionally gets tough.

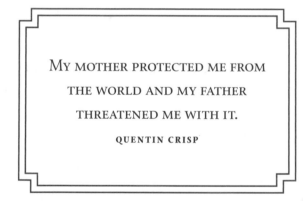

MY MOTHER PROTECTED ME FROM
THE WORLD AND MY FATHER
THREATENED ME WITH IT.

QUENTIN CRISP

LUNCH WITH LENNY

STEPHEN D. BOYD AS TOLD TO LANITA BRADLEY BOYD

"Who told you?" Josh asked belligerently, not even pretending to be contrite. "Who tattled?"

"Listen to me, young man! Parents have sources you don't even dream of. How we found out is beside the point—we're just disappointed that you would torture another kid like that. Have your mother and I taught you *nothing*?" I was on a rampage.

My wife jumped right in. "Son, you know you should be kind to everyone, but especially kids like Lenny. We're going to have to think of an appropriate punishment for this. Do you have any ideas?"

Josh muttered something about not being the only one involved and suggested apologizing to Lenny.

"Well, of course!" I said. "But that's the tip of the iceberg. You need to do something to really make it up to Lenny for being so mean to him today—and other days, I suspect. I think the punishment should fit the crime."

My children were both blessed and cursed by having their mother teach in their elementary school. Whereas it was a convenient fix for things like a forgotten field trip signature, having her know too much about their school lives did not balance the scales in their estimations. This time, her insider information worked to Lenny's advantage.

"Josh, your mom tells me that she often sees Lenny sitting alone to eat at lunchtime. Does he have any friends?" I asked.

"No. Who would want to be his friend? He's so dumb, Dad! You don't understand!"

"No, I don't. But soon you're going to. I think you need to overtly offer him your friendship."

Josh scowled. He could tell that whatever was coming would not be fun.

The solution continued to take form in my mind. "I think you need to eat lunch with Lenny and talk to him like you would your other friends. How about that?" I suggested. His eyes widened in horror. I was onto something.

"Let's quantify it," I said. "Let's say you eat lunch with Lenny three times a week for a month. That should help you and him both. You'll start tomorrow."

Josh had no choice. The following day, his mom

scanned the cafeteria as she entered. Sure enough, there was Josh, sitting with Lenny, both eating silently. I had to chuckle when she told me. Poor Lenny was probably wondering what Josh was up to.

Josh saw her enter and remembered the rules—I had added that if she observed him being rude and not conversational, then that day wouldn't count toward the twelve he had to put in. She saw his mouth move quickly as he started talking to Lenny.

Most weeks, Josh went with Monday, Wednesday, Friday. Once he tried three days in a row to get it over with, but he decided a break between days worked better in dealing with Lenny.

His teacher didn't take long to pick up on the situation. She came into the teacher's lunchroom, laughing. "You are the meanest parents I have ever known!" she told my wife. "I can't imagine a worse punishment than sitting with Lenny Colvin!"

And I knew she was right. It was a tough punishment. But more and more, I was convinced we'd done the right thing. Over the next month, while Josh and Lenny didn't exactly become bosom buddies, a truce was both declared and enacted.

When Lenny's family moved away later that year, Josh did not share the glee of the other students. "Lenny really did have a hard life, Dad," he commented when he told me Lenny had moved. I took that offhand comment as a sign that our "punishment" had been effective.

How do we ever know what punishment is best? As a parent, I constantly struggle with discipline. When should I be firm and resolute? When should I show mercy? If I go the "tough" route, how tough should I be? If I show mercy, am I failing to give my kids the structure and limits they need?

And so, as my kids grow up, I pray for wisdom, for help to know what will stunt their spiritual or social development and what will nurture it. God, of course, is a vast resource of parenting wisdom, and I have confidence that He'll clue me in as situations arise. ◆

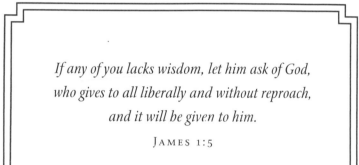

If any of you lacks wisdom, let him ask of God,
who gives to all liberally and without reproach,
and it will be given to him.

JAMES 1:5

TOUGH GUYS OF THE BIBLE

Next time you're facing a situation that requires toughness on your part, take a look at these biblical tough guys for inspiration and encouragement:

- David. Harp notwithstanding, David showed undeniable toughness in facing down predators both animal and human. His toughness in defending his sheep and God's name was part of what made him "a man after God's own heart" (1 Samuel 13:14).
- John the Baptist. A bit of a rogue, Jesus' cousin was His forerunner, the one who issued a bold call to repentance to all who awaited the coming Kingdom. He also spoke out against the king for his unlawful relationship with his brother's wife.
- Joseph. In Joseph's lifetime, he was sold into slavery, worked for the king, resisted temptation even though it cost him his job, and reached out with forgiveness to the family members who betrayed him. His diligence made him an icon of faith for ages to come.

What these godly tough guys all have in common is their commitment to follow the Lord and fight for right at all costs. Take heart: As you commit to serve God by serving your kids' highest good, you'll receive from Him the same strength and resolve He gave these men of faith. ◆

Zeal for your house will consume me.

JOHN 2:17B NIV

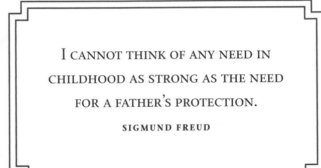

I CANNOT THINK OF ANY NEED IN
CHILDHOOD AS STRONG AS THE NEED
FOR A FATHER'S PROTECTION.

SIGMUND FREUD

The Everlasting Arms

MARGARET LANG

I grew up in my dad's loving arms. True, I spent most of my time playing with my friends and my dog, but it was my dad's hugs that took up the most space in my heart.

When Dad first got home from work, I would jump into his arms and get a squeeze. After dinner, I would snuggle in his arms on his soft lap. The next morning, I would cuddle in his arms on the edge of his bed.

I discovered something else about my dad's embrace. It also provided my best refuge from danger.

A city family, every summer we visited our Southern farm with its vast expanse of forest, meadow, and bayou. As any curious child would, I tried to make friends with each strange creature I encountered.

When I was five, I climbed under a fence rail to pet the "pretty tail" connected to a huge bull. Somehow without disturbing the animal, Dad's soft voice gently wooed me out of the pen and into the safety of his arms.

At six, accustomed to my graceful, well-groomed collie, I was intrigued by a limping, bedraggled mutt. As I stroked him, he lifted his drooping head, not to lick me as I had hoped, but to bite me. Dad held me in his strong arms for the painful shots.

As a seven-year-old playing by a pond, I was inches away from sitting on the head of what I thought was a statue of an alligator. When its jaws opened to take a bite out of me, fear jet-propelled me right back into my dad's loving arms.

So having survived to age eight, I felt indestructible when my older brother and I mounted horses to ride slowly along the dusty farm roads. After all, I knew my dad would always be around to catch me.

When we turned in the direction of the barn, our ride done for the day, my horse decided he was in a hurry to get home. Without warning, he took off running, his mane blowing and my pigtails flying.

"Pull back on the reins!" my brother yelled.

The reins? I looked around for them. Too late. I had let them drop out of reach so both my hands would be free to clutch the saddle horn.

The louder I screamed, the faster the horse ran. With my brother left in the dust behind me and the barn way ahead, I was alone in a no-man's land—without Dad.

If only he were here to rescue me. I felt so vulnerable. I gripped the horn until my knuckles blanched, but even so my body still bounced in the saddle like a Raggedy Ann doll. Each second of every minute, I felt like I would bounce off.

Then I saw it, the high wooden farm gate looming ahead. But the gate was closed, forming a barrier between my horse and the barn where he was headed.

I'd seen enough cowboy movies to be pretty sure this wild ride was not going to end as gracefully as a Gene Autry scene. Instinctively, I knew that whether my horse jumped the gate or stopped suddenly in front of it, either way, I was about to be launched like a Fourth of July rocket.

"Help!" I screamed over and over. Unaware the cinch was loose and the saddle beneath me was slipping, I sensed that I was sliding off the horse. I squeezed the horse's sides with both my thighs, hugged his back with my body—and hung on for dear life.

My horse approached the gate at full speed and the dusty wind stung my face. And then, through half-closed eyes, I saw my dad. He was running to reach the other side of the gate, and like a stop-motion movie, his long strides looked to me like they were hitting the ground in slow motion. He took hold of the gate and violently shoved it open—just in the nick of time. My horse and I brushed past Dad and flew through the gate.

When the lathered horse slowed down and came to a stop at the barn, I slid off onto the ground, crying. In a moment, my loving dad swept me up into his secure arms. How safe I felt—like nothing could ever harm me again.

Amazing how I carried over that childhood sense of security in my dad's arms right into my adult trust in my Heavenly Father's embrace. I thank God for dads who know how to be fierce in protecting and fierce in loving their kids, how to hug the love and comfort of God right into their children's souls. ◆

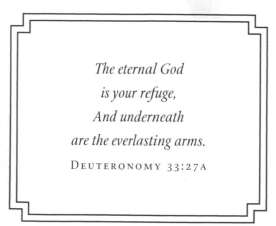

*The eternal God
is your refuge,
And underneath
are the everlasting arms.*

DEUTERONOMY 33:27A

WHEN TO GET TOUGH

Toughness needs to be applied judiciously—there's a right time and way for toughness to be expressed. Thankfully, God offers us His wisdom in abundance and helps us figure out how and when to get tough.

Take some time today to pray and ask God to help you cultivate the right kind of toughness. Pray for wisdom with which to evaluate the situations you're facing; ask God to cultivate in you His tough, yet tender heart; bring your kids before the Lord and pray that they would experience God's tough love through you.

As you pray and commit your parenting to the Lord, rest assured that you're well on your way to becoming the father God created you to be. ◆

For the LORD gives wisdom;
From His mouth come
knowledge and understanding.

PROVERBS 2:6

God's Promises for Standing Firm

In repentance and rest is your salvation,
in quietness and trust is your strength.

ISAIAH 30:15B NIV

It is God who arms me with strength,
And makes my way perfect.

PSALM 18:32

God began doing a good work in you,
and I am sure he will continue it until
it is finished when Jesus Christ comes again.

PHILIPPIANS 1:6 NCV

Now it is God who makes both us
and you stand firm in Christ.

2 CORINTHIANS 1:21A NIV

Therefore, as the elect of God,
holy and beloved, put on tender mercies,
kindness, humility, meekness, longsuffering.

COLOSSIANS 3:12

REAL MEN ARE GENTLE

It's true that kids need a strong dad; but truly great strength often takes the form of gentleness. And that tenderness is what makes kids feel safe, protected, and abundantly loved.

Gentleness puts a Band-Aid on a scrape, consoles a recently-defeated ballplayer, and reaches out with strong, tender arms to hug a prodigal. Best of all, when we show gentleness, we're modeling ourselves after our Father in heaven.

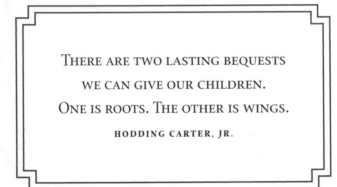

THERE ARE TWO LASTING BEQUESTS
WE CAN GIVE OUR CHILDREN.
ONE IS ROOTS. THE OTHER IS WINGS.

HODDING CARTER, JR.

IF YOU'RE GONNA QUIT, DON'T TELL DADDY!

MAX DAVIS

I'm almost certain that the day I popped into this world, my dad was standing right there in the delivery room with a football in his hands, anxiously waiting. As soon as the doc slapped my little round behind, Dad thrust the ball into my hands, patted my back, and said, "Go get 'em, tiger!"

A farmer's son, he grew up milking cows at 3:30 every morning and again at 4:30 every afternoon and never got the chance to play ball, even though he badly wanted to. So I guess the next best thing was a son he could live his dream through. As a result, I played seventeen years of football—from the third grade all the way through college, followed by an appalling tryout in the old USFL.

It must be said here, however, that my dad never forced me. He let it be known early that it was my decision to play, not his. But you know, I really wanted to please him and that made me work just a little bit harder—or a lot harder. When most kids were flipping burgers or serving up snow cones, I was running stadiums and lifting weights. I worked for my Dad's air conditioning business in the summers, but he made sure I went home early every afternoon to work out for football. My senior year of high school, Dad told me he'd give me $100 for every touchdown I scored. His motivation must have worked: I scored twenty-two TD's that year, setting a school record and racking up $2,200 in the process!

And did I mention that my dad was at every single game I ever played and almost every practice? I came to depend on him being present. Before a game, my stomach would be in knots, but as soon as I spotted him in the stands, a calm would wash over me and I was ready to play. I guess all my hard work along with my dad's motivation and support paid off, because I was fortunate enough to get a full-ride athletic scholarship to the University of Mississippi.

Oh, had I made Dad proud. And have mercy on your soul if you happened to run into him at the town's little coffee shop. Every word out of his mouth was "my boy" this and "my boy" that. Yes, sir, I had made my Dad some kind of proud. So you can imagine what happened on the day that I did the unthinkable: I quit the team.

I wasn't getting the playing time that I thought I deserved and I wasn't happy. Plus, I was having a rough time in general. So one morning at about 4:00, I packed my bags, sneaked out of the dorm, and quit—throwing away my scholarship and along with it all those years of dreams and hard work.

My home was six hours south, and because I knew how disappointed and angry Dad was going to be, I did the only thing I knew to do—drive north. So that's what I did. I drove due north on I-55 for over six hours.

Terrified, with tears blurring my vision, I had a lump in the pit of my stomach—that uneasy feeling you get when you know you have made a big mistake. The whole drive I was beating myself up thinking, *What are you going to do with your life? You've just thrown away your scholarship.* The tears flowed like rivers down my cheeks.

Finally, at some point near the outskirts of St. Louis, I realized there really was only one thing to do. I had to go home and face my fears—mainly Dad. I whipped my 1979 Monte Carlo around and drove twelve hours south to Baton Rouge.

Worn out and ragged from my emotional turmoil, not to mention an eighteen-hour drive, I at last turned onto

Leadale Drive. It was about ten o'clock at night, and from the street I could see the light on in the living room and knew that Mama and Dad were sitting there watching TV.

Scared senseless, I just drove around the block for I don't know long until I finally mustered up enough courage to knock on the door. When I did and Mama answered, I burst into the house crying, not because I quit football, not because I was going to miss it, not because I had thrown away a full scholarship, but because I knew how much I had let my dad down. I sat there in the middle of the living room floor repeating over and over again, "I quit the team! I'm such an idiot!"

For the longest time, Dad didn't say a word. He just sat in his La-Z-Boy and rocked quietly, pondering the situation. Finally, Mama broke the silence. "Jimmy!" she said. "Do something! Can't you see your son is in trouble?" (I always was "his" son when I messed up.)

Me, I was fully expecting to get railed on—for Dad to yell and carry on, say something to the tune of, "Yes, you are an idiot! You really blew it!"

But Dad didn't do anything of the sort. Instead, he looked up from his chair and in a soft tone of compassion said, "Son, there's only one thing we can do."

I wiped a tear from my face and asked, "What is that?"

"We have to go tomorrow and ask Coach Sloan to take you back."

"I can't go back!" I protested. "They'll never take me. Plus they'll laugh me back off campus!"

"Son, I know it's going to be hard, but this is something we have to do," he said. "And I'll go with you. Now, go take a shower and get some rest, and then in the morning we'll go."

I tossed and turned in bed that night, yet I had a strange peace that came with the unexpected and compassionate support of my dad. When morning arrived, after one of Mama's killer breakfasts, we got in my car and drove the six hours north to Oxford, Mississippi.

You know, during that whole drive, Dad never once put me down or belittled me, and as far as I could tell he didn't act disappointed in me. Instead of a six-hour lecture, that drive became one of the most powerful bonding times between my dad and me that I can remember.

When we finally made it to the coach's office, Dad looked up at me and said, "Okay, son, this is something you have to do. I can't go in for you."

I was shaking pretty hard, but Dad rubbed my

shoulder, calming me and giving me courage. I went in, faced the coach, and to my shock, he took me back. That afternoon, my dad took a bus home. What a dad!

I went on to finish my four years on full scholarship and graduated with a degree in journalism. It wasn't until over twenty-something years later, looking back, that I saw with clarity what an incredible act of wisdom and love my dad showed me that day. The experience helped me to grasp God's grace—because of my dad's love, I was able to hear God say to me again and again in the years to come, "Come on, son. I know you messed up. But come on and get in the car with Me. I'll go with you and support you and help you overcome what you're going through."

If my Dad had condemned and belittled me, chances are I would not have gone back and finished my education. Criticism and belittling bind people, grace frees them. And I'm grateful to my dad—and to my God—for the grace that has freed me and made my life wonderful. ◆

Where God's love is, there is no fear,
because God's perfect love drives out fear.
It is punishment that makes a person fear,
so love is not made perfect in the person who fears.

1 JOHN 4:18 NCV

Dad Hugs

Sometimes it's hard to show affection. But if we're willing to make the effort to encourage and affirm our kids both verbally and physically, studies show that we'll make our kids more secure, more self-confident, and less likely to have social and emotional problems. In other words, a few well placed hugs and words of encouragement make our kids more able to face the world. And that's the goal of every dad.

*Your love has given me great
joy and encouragement.*

PHILEMON 1:7A NIV

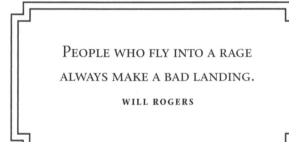

PEOPLE WHO FLY INTO A RAGE
ALWAYS MAKE A BAD LANDING.

WILL ROGERS

The Rules of Engagement

JAY COOKINGHAM

The situation was tense. On one side was a very angry civilian, on the other side a senior officer with superior firepower behind him. There was shouting, then threats, and soon the senior officer let his anger get the best of him and forgot the rules of engagement, speaking and acting unkindly. The civilian reacted with his own angry conduct, and the situation boiled over. I (the senior officer) had blown it—I had provoked my son to anger.

It all started when I asked my ten-year-old son, Mike, if he had finished his chores. I knew that he left them half finished and was now distracted by video games. When he answered my inquiry with a mumbled "I don't know," the battle lines were drawn.

"Excuse me?" I asked. "You don't know if you finished your chores? Just who would know that information, then?"

Shrugging his shoulders, his eyes wandered to avoid mine and the tension surged between us. "I guess I'm finished. . . Besides, it was my turn to play and I wanted to play," Mike replied sharply.

"So, playing video games became more important than answering me honestly? Is that true?" I asked, my voice now growing louder.

Mike became very quiet.

"Well, Mike, is it? I'm waiting for an answer!" My voice was louder still.

Mike was still quiet, but now glaring at me. Communication was rapidly breaking down but instead of calling for a translator (my wife) I started to read him the riot act. I was yelling now, telling how disrespectful he was being and how dare he and who did he think he was—I had lost containment.

After a few minutes of ranting, I finally asked him, "Well, do you have anything to say?"

His tone dark with frustration, Mike replied, "Not when you're yelling at me I don't!"

He was angry. And that's when I realized that I had caused my son to sin.

In my own anger I had caused my son to break the first commandment: honoring your mother and father. I had used my own authority in a very un-gentle display of "I'll show you who's the boss," causing him to get angry. I remembered the verse from Ephesians—"And you, fathers, do not provoke your children to wrath, but bring them up in the training and admonition of the Lord" (6:4)—and I felt terrible.

In a moment of anger, I had completely disregarded what I had come to consider God's standing rules of engagement for my life. In the military, standing rules of engagement are directives that define the framework for actions and attitude of soldiers in critical situations. As I'd grown as a father, my Heavenly Father had taught me about how to conduct myself as I interacted with my kids—how to "bring them up in the training and admonition of the Lord."

As I studied the Fruits of the Spirit from Galatians— "But the fruit of the Spirit is love, joy, peace, longsuffering, kindness, goodness, faithfulness, gentleness, self-control" (5:22–23a)—I saw that those traits epitomize the way the Father relates to us as His children. One of the greatest characteristics of God is His gentleness. How often He had dealt with me gently and tenderly as my Father! I knew that gentleness was His standard to follow in all situations, especially in the training of our children.

Gentleness doesn't mean weakness; it usually requires more strength to be gentle and kind than to be mean. And

I had been a little mean with Mike. I'd forgotten to feast on the fruit of gentleness, a fruit that helps us to be angry and yet not sin. I knew I had to repent, so I went to Mike and asked for his forgiveness. I told him I was sorry I had lost my cool and allowed the situation to escalate the way it did. I told him I knew God had a better way for us to interact together.

Anytime I've messed up with my kids, I've found asking for forgiveness to be a very fruitful way to handle the situation. It may take a while to process, but our Father promises to help us and guide us, and His gentleness and grace toward us makes all the difference.

How do I know this? When my son forgave me that day, I felt the strength of our relationship grow and the distance between us fade away. ◆

Fathers, do not provoke your children to anger
by the way you treat them. Rather, bring them up with
the discipline and instruction that comes from the Lord.

EPHESIANS 6:4B NLT

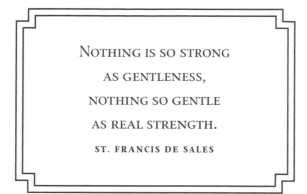

NOTHING IS SO STRONG
AS GENTLENESS,
NOTHING SO GENTLE
AS REAL STRENGTH.

ST. FRANCIS DE SALES

*Let everyone see that
you are gentle and kind.*

PHILIPPIANS 4:5A NCV

God's Promises for Cultivating a Tender Heart

*For whom He foreknew, He also predestined
to be conformed to the image of His Son, that
He might be the firstborn among many brethren.*

ROMANS 8:29

Love will cover a multitude of sins.

1 PETER 4:8B

A soft answer turns away wrath.

PROVERBS 15:1A

Don't repay evil for evil. Don't retaliate with insults when people insult you. Instead, pay them back with a blessing. That is what God has called you to do, and he will bless you for it.

1 PETER 3:9 NLT

The lowly will possess the land and will live in peace and prosperity.

PSALM 37:11 NLT

If we love one another, God abides in us,
and His love has been perfected in us.

1 JOHN 4:12B

REAL MEN SHOW THE LOVE OF GOD

When we realize how much we love our kids, it shocks us a little to realize that God loves us the same way—but even more. We've been given an awesome task, responsibility, and privilege: to show our kids the love of God.

Every time we show patience, set limits, and make our kids feel loved, we're laying the groundwork for them to have a great relationship with God. And when we model our fathering after that of God the Father, we're becoming the very best fathers we can be.

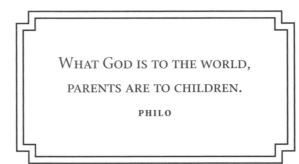

WHAT GOD IS TO THE WORLD,
PARENTS ARE TO CHILDREN.

PHILO

THE NAİL

MAX DAVIS

My daughter Kristen's tenth birthday party started out happy and normal. What could go wrong at a child's birthday party, right? But just as the party was in full swing, the unimaginable happened.

Some relatives had helped us decorate, hanging balloons all around the front porch on nails that had been driven securely into the wood to hang potted plants. One of the balloons was the thick latex type, with a heavy-duty rubber band attached—the kind that you bounce back and forth off your knuckles while holding the rubber band.

As the scenario unfolded, my son, James, wanted a balloon—not just any balloon, but that balloon. It was within his reach, so he grabbed it and did what any eight-year-old would do. He started pulling. But the rubber band was attached to the nail and wouldn't come down. The more James pulled, the tighter the rubber band stretched. Then, in a microsecond, the nail was dislodged. The force of the stretched rubber band bulleted the nail directly into James' chest, embedding it there. You can imagine our shock as James came stumbling into the living room, stunned, with a three-inch nail driven into his chest.

It was not a pretty sight. The nail had projected through his bone and was driven so deep that we thought he might die. We were scared to move him because we didn't know if the nail had hit an artery or a lung or what. Someone called 911. Soon an ambulance and fire truck filled our front lawn. Lights were flashing everywhere. Cars were slowing down on the street to inquire. Kristen's birthday cake and presents lay untouched as the paramedics worked intensely. The girls were crying. The paramedics secured James so he could not move, slid him into the ambulance, and whisked him away as my father-in-law and I followed. They would not allow me to ride in the ambulance with my own son. James watched in terror, screaming for me to come, but all I could do was watch.

You see, my son is totally deaf. What must have gone through his mind during that ambulance ride? *Why has Daddy left me? Why won't he come?*

At the hospital, the X-rays revealed that the nail had barely missed an artery and was resting on his lung. Mercifully, it had not punctured it. The ER doctor's words went like this: "It is evident that Someone upstairs is watching over your son, because if that nail had lodged a half-inch in either direction, he would be dead. Or the nail could have hit his eye or gone into his head."

I was ready to get my son out of there. The doctor told me, "We could put him under anesthesia and do surgery to remove the nail, but for someone as young as James, that might cause further complications. We need to get the nail out now." Then he looked me in the eye and said, "It's going to be painful. But it's for the best."

James was given pain medication, but it had little effect and he was screaming. The doctor instructed me to hold my son down while he attempted to remove the nail. Soon we realized that this was going to be a much more difficult task than we had first thought.

Each time the doctor merely touched the nail, the pain would send James jerking and screaming. The doctor took a pair of pliers and started pulling the nail, but it wouldn't budge. It was driven in his chest like a nail hammered into a piece of lumber. Because of his deafness, James couldn't talk, but the whole time his eyes were locked onto mine. They pierced through me and said it all: *Daddy, do something. Don't let the doctor hurt me. Please, Daddy, please.*

I too was in tears and, in a moment of weakness, I let go.

The doctor sternly confronted me and said I had to be strong and hold him down. "It's for his own good," he reminded me again. Despite knowing what was best, holding my son down was one of the hardest things I've ever had to do. I also knew that I had within me the authority to stop the whole procedure and request surgery. My instincts as a father, however, told me that this was the best thing to do in the long run.

So I took a deep breath and once again wrapped my arms around James and held him down—this time more tightly than before. The whole time his eyes never stopped speaking to me: *Dad, how could you betray me, you of all people? I trusted you. You know how this is hurting me. Daddy, I'm in pain. Do something!*

Yet all I could do was hold him down. This time, the doctor literally straddled James and pulled with his arms using his legs for more power. That's how deeply lodged the nail was. Finally, after what seemed an eternity, the nail popped out. James and I sat there, in a pile of sweat, exhausted and emotionally spent. The pain subsided. The distress was over.

James looked at me as if to say, "Daddy, why did you

let them do that to me?" All I could do was hold him in my arms and love him. He couldn't understand why I had done what I did, and words wouldn't matter right then. He would understand when he got older, I thought—I hoped.

Yes, my son was hurting, and I was hurting for him. Only another parent can know the torment I was going through. But I realized something. Just as God has the power to step into our lives and say "enough is enough," I too had the power to stop James' pain. Yet I knew to do so would ultimately be even more harmful to him; it was my love for him that enabled me to do what was best for him. That day, I think I came to understand something about God's love, how it stays beside us and holds us up even in the midst of our pain.

As we drove home, I took comfort in knowing that James was going to get better—and that just as I hurt for my son, God hurts for us. ◆

> *The LORD is close to the brokenhearted,*
> *and saves those who are crushed in spirit.*
>
> PSALM 34:18 NIV

LOVE DIVINE

God is the ultimate loving Father.

- He guides us (Psalm 32:8)
- He meets our needs (Matthew 6:26)
- He tenderly cares for us and leads us (Isaiah 40:11)
- He disciplines us (Hebrews 12:10)
- He sings over us (Zephaniah 3:17)

When we have kids, we experience a new understanding of the love of God; we suddenly see ourselves as loved by Him the way we love our kids. As you pray for the ability to love your kids divinely, include a prayer of thanks for God's amazing, life-changing love for you. ◆

As a father has compassion
on his children,
so the Lord has compassion
on those who fear him.

PSALM 103:13 NIV

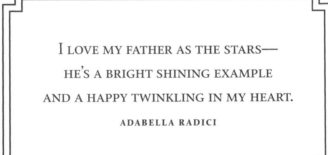

I LOVE MY FATHER AS THE STARS—
HE'S A BRIGHT SHINING EXAMPLE
AND A HAPPY TWINKLING IN MY HEART.

ADABELLA RADICI

Come and Fish

SHARON HINCK

"Let's go fishing."

Each time my dad offered that invitation, my heart raced like a lure flashing through the water. My most evocative memories of Dad center on afternoons of waiting for the Big One to bite. The sputter of an outboard motor and the slap of waves against an aluminum hull still raise my pulse.

As I grew up, I cherished each rare fishing trip. Dad was an on-the-go executive who traveled a lot. But when we fished, we both surrendered to the peace of a sun-soaked Minnesota lake. It was our special time. Anticipation built while I watched my bobber float and listened to ducks calling to each other in the reeds. When my rod gave an exhilarating tug, I relished the battle of reeling in a sunfish, no matter how tiny the catch.

Dad would congratulate me and add the fish to our stringer. Then he'd tell me about the huge northern pike and walleye he had caught on his fishing trips in Canada.

He promised that when I was older, he'd take me along one day for some serious fishing.

But years swam past. I battled the challenges of adolescence. He battled cancer. And sometimes we battled each other.

I left for college, got engaged, and my fiancé became the primary man in my life. The next summer, home for vacation, I sat at the kitchen counter making a cheese sandwich. Dad came in from cleaning the garage and poured himself a glass of buttermilk.

I spread mayonnaise on my bread. "So, Dad. Next summer I'll be married."

He nodded. "Yep. Hard to believe."

"And we never took that big fishing trip together."

He set his glass down. "You still like fishing?"

"It's been a while. But, yeah. I still want to try my hand at landing a northern."

He rubbed his hand over his crew cut and cleared his throat. "Let's do it."

That weekend, we made the long drive north to Lake of the Woods on the Canadian border. We rented a musty cabin and stocked up on Kit Kats and Coke. The next morning we headed out through pre-dawn mist on our quest to do some serious fishing.

The scent of gasoline from the motor mingled with the tang of Coppertone—an alluring combination that promised adventure.

We motored along the shore and stopped in promising coves to cast for a while. My lure kept tangling in the weeds, and Dad patiently helped me pull it free so I could cast again.

By the time the sun was fully up, I felt my first strike. I cranked and played the fish while Dad coached me. The northern pike was a more demanding foe than the sunfish and perch of my youth. I teased it closer to the boat, and Dad stood up with the net. The boat rocked. My rod arced from the strain. Dad swooped the net, and a long, gleaming pike flopped in the bottom of our boat.

"This one's a beauty," Dad proclaimed.

It was a proud moment. Dad had invited me into his world and I proved I could catch the big ones, just like he did. Suddenly Dad's fishing rod jumped, and it was my turn to grab the net. I helped him land his catch, and the fish kept us busy the rest of the afternoon.

I still have the photo that Dad took of me at the end of our day of fishing. In the snapshot, I'm wearing a stained bandana over my hair and a red flannel shirt. My nose is pink from not using enough sunscreen. I'm holding a stringer of northern that I could barely lift, and my grin is so huge it makes my eyes squint.

That was the last fishing trip Dad and I took together. The next summer, he walked me down the aisle at my wedding. Three years later, he lost his battle with cancer.

That day of fishing stands out in my mind as a perfect memory of Dad, a memory of him sharing one of his greatest pleasures with me and giving me a glimpse of his pride in me. It's a memory that reflects God's love in my life.

Because of those fishing trips, I know how wonderful it feels to have my Father in the boat with me. He may have to bait my hook and untangle my line. But He still smiles on me with pleasure. His is a love that guides me and challenges me and keeps me safe, all at the same time. And I learned the power of that kind of love from my dad. ◆

For great is your love,
reaching to the heavens;
your faithfulness
reaches to the skies.

PSALM 57:10 NIV

FROM "VIOLIN SONGS: LOVE IS HOME"

BY GEORGE MACDONALD

Faithful creator, heart-longed-for father,
Home of our heart-infolded brother,
Home to thee all thy glories gather—
All are thy love, and there is no other!
O Love-at-rest, we loves that roam—
Home unto thee, we are coming home!

HOME IS THE FIRST SCHOOL
AND THE FIRST CHURCH WHERE
WE LEARN ABOUT LOVING GOD.

ERNESTINE SCHUMANN-HEINK

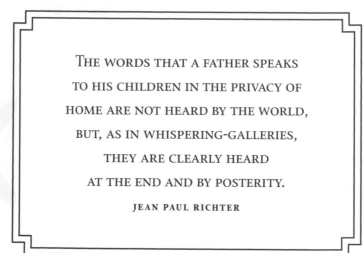

THE WORDS THAT A FATHER SPEAKS
TO HIS CHILDREN IN THE PRIVACY OF
HOME ARE NOT HEARD BY THE WORLD,
BUT, AS IN WHISPERING-GALLERIES,
THEY ARE CLEARLY HEARD
AT THE END AND BY POSTERITY.

JEAN PAUL RICHTER

WORDS

SALLY CLARK

Words are powerful creations. The words we write can live on long after we die, waiting in books and papers to come to life in other minds. The words we say can hang in the air like yellowed leaves waiting for a gusting wind to send them on their way. But the words we hear can become a part of us, buried away, deep in our memories, forgotten but never gone.

My dad spoke words into my life. When I was a little girl, every evening was a frenzy of tickling, giggling, and coaxing me into bed. When playtime was finally done and I was successfully lying in my pink-trimmed sheets, the tucking-in began. The overhead light that had laughed over our roughhousing went out, and the nightlight went on, pushing the shadows away. Daddy's voice turned serious and his eyes peered into mine in the semi-darkness.

"Who loves you, little girl?" he asked.

"You and Mommy," I answered.

"That's right. And don't you forget it," Daddy would say, using his serious voice, bending to kiss my cheek. And trusting the words I heard, I closed my eyes and drifted off to sleep.

As the years went by, the bedtime ritual changed. I took my bath and snuggled under the covers with Nancy Drew, having outgrown the tickling and tumbling. As I flicked on my reading light, Daddy stood in my bedroom doorway and asked the question that was beginning to annoy me. Of course I knew my mom and dad loved me. What else would they do? The question seemed childish.

I rolled to my side and said, "I know, I know—you and Mom. G'night, Daddy. I love you too."

Still more changes came. Now I sat on the side of the bed and polished my toenails while Daddy asked, "Who loves you, little girl?"

"I'm not a little girl, Daddy," I answered.

"I'm still asking."

"You and Mother," I sighed, concentrating on the "Pink Passion" moving from the bottom of my toenail to the top.

"That's right. Don't forget."

But I did forget. Not intentionally, just neglect-fully, taking my father's love for granted; not thinking it anything to treasure, but something common to all children. And I buried the bedtime tradition in my memories, like the Cinderella bedspread Mother made for my room and the swing set Daddy anchored in concrete in the back yard.

Why did he repeat those words every night, creating a sacrament that became so ordinary I took it for granted? Maybe he knew some people would come into my life who would not love me, and I would need the strength and grounding his words would give me. Maybe he knew that in the years ahead of me, I would need to remember where I belonged and to whom. Maybe he knew that being loved would give me a sense of value and worth. Whatever his intent, his words painted a picture for me of God's love and faithfulness.

Despite teenage rebellion and foolish behavior, my dad continued to love me, in action, in words, and in listening, just like God. And when I was an adult, overwhelmed with children and life and trying to survive, I remembered the words I heard as a child, and began to believe that God did love me, just like my father. When I needed my Dad's words the most, they were there, waiting for me, in my memories. And when I needed God's words the most, they were waiting for me too, in Scripture.

Sometimes the simplest things are the most profound. Those simple exchanges with my dad buried themselves in my heart. And there, they nurtured my soul and drew me to my Father. ◆

As a tree gives fruit, healing words give life.

PROVERBS 15:4A NCV

God's Promises for Reflecting His Love

By this all will know that you are My disciples,
if you have love for one another.

JOHN 13:35

He will turn the hearts of the fathers to
their children, and the hearts
of the children to their fathers.

MALACHI 4:6A NIV

And as we live in God, our love grows more perfect.

1 JOHN 4:17A NLT

Above all, clothe yourselves with love,
which binds us all together in perfect harmony.

COLOSSIANS 3:14 NLT

We also have joy with our troubles,
because we know that these troubles
produce patience. And patience produces
character, and character produces hope.
And this hope will never disappoint us,
because God has poured out his
love to fill our hearts.

ROMANS 5:3–5A NCV

REAL MEN HANG IN THERE

When it comes to parenting, you have to take the bad days with the good. There are days when things just go wrong; when your two-year-old refuses to do anything, the car breaks down—again—and your teenager doesn't want anything to do with you.

On days like these, a little perseverance is in order. And perseverance is easier when we remember the good days and anticipate better days ahead; when we keep in mind that our parenting efforts are paying dividends we may not see right now; and when we pray for strength.

Hang in there. God is on your side.

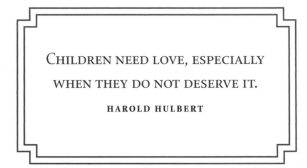

CHILDREN NEED LOVE, ESPECIALLY
WHEN THEY DO NOT DESERVE IT.

HAROLD HULBERT

Just Love Her

BARBARA M. HALLER

With clenched fists she stomped through the toddler years. Our little Katie was a courageous climber: up the stairs and out of a crib before she could walk, scrambling onto tables and kitchen counters.

With a steel will, our determined daughter had no intention of conforming to the expectations of anyone, especially me. She insisted on wearing her socks inside out, and with arms crossed she sternly told me at the shoe store that I would "be wasting money buying those shoes because I'm not going to wear them."

Katie scribbled precious, primitive notes to me, threatening to run away from a life made miserable by three bothersome big brothers. "But I know you'd miss me," was her tender postscript.

Some nights as I lay in bed, a sense of defeat enveloped me. I knew God should have the victory in this battle with Katie's will. But I stubbornly thought that God fully trusted me to do the job. I cried to my husband Bill, "She drives me crazy. What should I do with her? Does she need more discipline, or less? Do I need to lighten up?"

"Just love her" was his three-word cure. How his quick fix annoyed me! To me, "just love her" was on a par with permissiveness.

In my mind, Bill had the easier end of the loving deal. The revelry started after dinner each evening as four kids romped with Dad in the family room. Diving off sofas and rolling in pillow piles, our children squealed with wild abandon as Bill led the charge through hours of fun.

On the weekends, I gladly turned Katie over to Bill. Ashamedly, I derived some secret satisfaction when my husband's calm demeanor was ruffled by our daughter's emotional tidal waves. Now he knew what I was up against all week. Though tense with frustration, somehow he could muster up his motto and "just love her." Her tears soon turned to giggles and I was left baffled.

One Saturday night Bill's love-cure was severely tested. As he filled our large tub with bubbles and bath toys, three-year-old Katie took her battle position. "Wash my hair? Make me!" she seemed to say.

"Katie, your hair needs to be washed," Bill told her firmly. He coaxed and teased to no avail. She would not be swayed by Daddy's usual tender tactics.

Soon the scene escalated into one of thrashing arms, flying bubbles, dripping walls, and one drenched daddy. Katie's shrieks reverberated throughout the house. I hoped the neighbors couldn't hear the commotion.

Determined to subdue her and accomplish the task at hand, Bill stripped off most of his clothing and climbed into the tub with our hysterical daughter.

From my spot in the hall I soon heard not one, but two people crying. Katie's howls mingled with the long, deep sobs of my husband. As I peered around the corner, I gasped to see the two of them sobbing and sopping wet. At last, our little girl had surrendered and leaned into her daddy, relieved to surrender to—and be comforted by—his strength.

I sighed with gratitude that I'd married a man with an amazing capacity to put aside his frustration and intensely love our willful daughter. The moment reminded me that God never gives up on us. He weeps over our disobedience and waits to enfold us in His loving arms. He accepts us even when we are obstinate, screaming, and thoroughly unlovable. God wants us to realize our utter helplessness and lean fully on His strength. Through our messiness and moping, our tirades and tantrums, He loves us. He just loves us.

Katie is now in high school and her tantrums are a distant memory. God used my daughter's willfulness to build in her the strength of character she needs to resist negative influences. We still have a few battles of the will, but in the end we all realize that God has the final say.

The love that Bill poured into Katie must have filled her to the brim. It spills out as she calls from her room each night at bedtime, "G'night, Mom and Dad. I love you!" ◆

Love patiently accepts all things.
It always trusts, always hopes,
and always remains strong.

1 CORINTHIANS 13:7 NCV

From "Thoughts of a Father"

BY EDGAR A. GUEST

How can I best express my life? Wherein does greatness lie?
How can I long remembrance win, since I am born to die?
Both fame and gold are selfish things; their charms may quickly flee,
But I'm the father of a boy who came to speak for me.

In him lies all I hope to be; his splendor shall be mine;
I shall have done man's greatest work if only he is fine.
If some day he shall help the world long after I am dead,
In all that men shall say of him my praises shall be said.

It matters not what I may win of fleeting gold or fame,
My hope of joy depends alone on what my boy shall claim.
My story must be told through him, for him I work and plan,
Man's greatest duty is to be the father of a man.

UNTIL YOU HAVE A SON OF YOUR OWN
YOU WILL NEVER KNOW THE SENSE OF
HONOR THAT MAKES A MAN WANT TO
BE MORE THAN HE IS AND TO PASS
SOMETHING GOOD AND HOPEFUL
INTO THE HANDS OF HIS SON.

KENT NERBURN

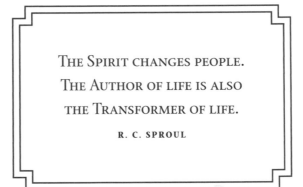

THE SPIRIT CHANGES PEOPLE.
THE AUTHOR OF LIFE IS ALSO
THE TRANSFORMER OF LIFE.

R. C. SPROUL

A Little Bit Better Than Yesterday

JEREMY MOORE

I once believed that nothing could silence a small group Bible study better than an invitation to close in prayer. But then I asked my men's group how family devotions worked in their own homes.

I got total silence.

I let the silence hang in the air for a while, and then learned that none of the dozen or so men around the table led what they thought were family devotions.

Yet all of them, I discovered, offered some sort of spiritual guidance, even if they didn't recognize it as such.

The term "family devotions" invokes images of husband, wife, and children sitting reverently around the dinner table, perhaps topped with a lace tablecloth and a few candles, as Dad dispenses spiritual truths from the Bible to his eager and expectant flock. That is a popular image, but it is also a fantasy. I know of no house where this actually happens.

"My kids are five, three, and one. I've got about a minute before one of them starts screaming," one father said. But although he offered this as an example of failure, what I heard was the story of a house where children received one more minute of spiritual instruction than they would receive in a house led by a man who cared not a whit about their souls.

Another man told the story of a time when he asked his daughters to pray for their mother, who had recently gone on a job interview. "I said, 'Let's pray for Mommy,' and they immediately went and kneeled by the ottoman." He was amazed—just like that, the family prayer he'd been trying to institute became a reality, simply because he was willing to make an effort to incorporate prayer into their daily lives. What might have happened if he had given up because their family prayer times weren't perfect?

I think sometimes we let the image of the perfect family devotion time become the enemy of the good we can do in our homes. If we can't do it perfectly, we think, why should we bother?

But God does not call us to be perfect. He calls us each day to be a little bit better than yesterday. As we follow and obey Him, who knows where our growth will take us?

Whether we see it immediately or not, our efforts are paying off. ◆

*Depend on the Lord
in whatever you do,
and your plans
will succeed.*

PROVERBS 16:3 NCV

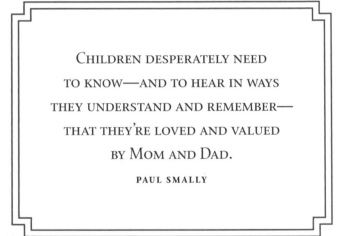

CHILDREN DESPERATELY NEED
TO KNOW—AND TO HEAR IN WAYS
THEY UNDERSTAND AND REMEMBER—
THAT THEY'RE LOVED AND VALUED
BY MOM AND DAD.

PAUL SMALLY

A Father's Call

STEPHEN D. BOYD AS TOLD TO LANITA BRADLEY BOYD

One Sunday morning as I pulled out of the church parking lot and onto the busy street, I heard a muffled sob from the back seat. "Kelsey, what's wrong?" I asked. Since she was on the home stretch of age fourteen, I wasn't surprised by her tears.

Sometime after her fifth or so teen drama, Kelsey and I developed a kind of routine we'd go through that often seemed to help. I would ask what was wrong, and she would say, "Nothing" (of course). And then I would persuade her to tell me who had so wronged her, at which point I would say sympathetically, "Would you like for me to talk to her?" (Or him. Usually him.)

Then she would look at me in horror and say, "*No!* Dad, please, *please* don't do that!" The vision of her dad talking to her friend or teacher about the problem at hand seemed so much worse than the actual problem that she would cheer up immediately. She finally had control over a part of the situation—the part that entailed me embarrassing her by paternally scolding a classmate. No more tears.

Unfortunately, this particular Sunday, our routine failed. Horribly.

As it turned out, she was really being persecuted. Patrick, a friend she'd known from church since birth, was constantly goading her and making fun of her, she said. "I always thought of him as my little brother," Kelsey cried. "And now he's so mean to me!"

I thought of how mean I often was to my older sister, which to me made Patrick seem more like a brother, not less, but I kept those thoughts to myself.

When prompted for specific examples, all she could come up with was "You think you're so smart because you're the preacher's daughter!" and "All the teachers like you because you suck up to them!" Then she added, hesitantly, "And he says mean things about Adam and me kissing and we didn't. He just embarrasses me all the time!"

"It's not so much what he says as how he never lets up," she went on. "There's hardly a pause between his insults. And of course he's really funny about it, so the other kids laugh, and that just feeds him to continue. I'm sick of it! I don't want to even go to church or teen group or anything as long as Patrick will be there!"

"Well, that's awful," I said mildly. "Since he doesn't have a sister, he may not realize how much it bothers you. Do you want me to talk to him? It's your call."

Silence. Finally, "Yes, I do. Maybe that would make a difference."

I was shocked. I was supposed to reprimand the son of one of our elders, one of my best friends? She'd really called my bluff this time.

When we got home, I allowed myself to think maybe she would just forget about the phone call if I laid low for a while. But that would be wrong. And so, being the diligent and consistent dad that I am, I went straight to my office and dialed Patrick's home number. (Although I guess it's possible that part of me hoped they hadn't made it home from church yet.)

But they had. His dad—my friend, my elder, the husband of one of my wife's best friends—answered the phone.

"Hey, Mike," I said, maybe a little too loudly. "Could I speak to Patrick?" Fortunately, Mike didn't seem to think much about it, since I often asked the teen boys to help with a worship service or a service project of some sort.

After a short pause, I heard Patrick's teenage hello. No turning back now and no sense beating around the bush.

"Patrick, I understand that you have been persecuting Kelsey, and I want it to stop," I said.

Another pause, Patrick's surprise crackling over the line. "Yes, sir," he squeaked.

"You and Kelsey have been friends for a lot of years now, and you are ruining that friendship," I continued. I couldn't believe I was saying this. I mean, I'm a pretty up-front, direct kind of guy, but I couldn't help but think this was just a little crazy. I thought of Kelsey and kept on. "You have her so upset that she doesn't even want to attend church when you are there. From now on I want you only to speak kind words to Kelsey. Anything you say to her must be positive and encouraging and never disparaging. Is that understood?"

"Yes, sir!" he said, with more emphasis than the first time.

"I hope we won't have to mention this again, Patrick," I added.

"No, we won't, sir!" he answered. I'd never heard "yes sir" so much in such a short span of time. I felt like a drill sergeant. For half a second, I entertained the idea of having him put his parents on the phone so I could compliment them on teaching their son good manners, but instantly dismissed that thought. This conversation would stay between the two of us.

When I joined the family for lunch, I told Kelsey that I'd talked to Patrick and her problems would cease. She threw her arms around me, thrilled, and I was touched at her confidence in the effect of one phone call from me. And she wasn't disappointed: From that day on, Patrick was incredibly kind and solicitous of Kelsey and her well-being.

When they ended up at the same college, their friendship continued on an adult level, with Kelsey acting as Patrick's advice-giving and loving older sister and Patrick in turn calling or stopping by her apartment for food, advice, games, or consolation as needed.

A couple of years later, when I saw Patrick sitting in a front-row pew at Kelsey's wedding, I had to chuckle at the memory of that call. I certainly never made that kind of phone call a habit; but I think every once in a while, a dad does something for his child without fully understanding it, and somehow things turn out for the best. ◆

Guide me in your truth and teach me, for you are God my Savior, and my hope is in you all day long.

PSALM 25:5 NIV

GOD'S PROMISES
FOR PERSEVERING

He gives strength to those who are tired
and more power to those who are weak.

ISAIAH 40:29 NCV

Come to Me, all you who labor and are heavy laden,
and I will give you rest. Take My yoke upon you and
learn from Me, for I am gentle and lowly in heart,
and you will find rest for your souls.
For My yoke is easy and My burden is light.

MATTHEW 11:28–30

So we don't look at the troubles we can see right now;
rather, we fix our gaze on things that cannot be seen.
For the things we see now will soon be gone,
but the things we cannot see will last forever.

2 CORINTHIANS 4:18 NLT

I can do all things through Christ,
because he gives me strength.

PHILIPPIANS 4:13 NCV

Keep on asking, and you will receive what you ask for.
Keep on seeking, and you will find.
Keep on knocking, and the door will be opened to you.

MATTHEW 7:7 NLT

> *Don't let your hearts be troubled.*
> *Trust in God, and trust also in me.*
>
> JOHN 14:1 NLT

REAL MEN KNOW WHEN TO LET GO

It's nice to be needed. We love it when our kids need our help fixing a toy or solving a math problem. But as our kids grow more and more independent, they need us a little less every day. And that stings a little.

We know, though, that it's best for our kids to separate from us and to find their wings. We know we need to let go a little at a time, even as we nurture our kids and provide them with a solid, loving base from which to launch.

We can take comfort in knowing that letting go doesn't mean leaving them to struggle on their own—we're entrusting them to a Father who loves them even more than we do. Remembering His love for us and for our kids makes letting go a lot easier.

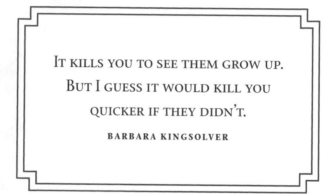

It kills you to see them grow up.
But I guess it would kill you
quicker if they didn't.

BARBARA KINGSOLVER

Starting Young

SHANE WERLINGER

"Hey, Shane, why don't you sit down?"

I looked at my wife, Sandy, like she was crazy. Sit down while Lauren played on the playscape? What if she fell and got hurt? What if another kid was mean to her? Didn't Sandy realize she'd just turned three years old?

"No thanks, sweetheart," I responded, coyly evading my wife's intention. "I'm not tired. I don't feel like sitting down."

I watched from the corner of my eye as Sandy approached the steps of the playscape. She gently touched my arm to stop me from fleeing to the bridge behind Lauren.

"Come on, Shane. Let's let her play by herself for a while and see what happens."

In my heart I knew she was right. As much as I wanted to hold Lauren's hand forever, I knew it would be good for her to explore her world a little on her own, with me standing close, but not too close. I had known this day was coming; sooner or later, I knew I would have to loosen my grip, a little bit at a time. But did it have to start today? She was just a baby.

I looked down into my beautiful daughter's face. She peered back with a look of excitement mixed with apprehension. The excitement was winning out.

"Okay," I sighed, releasing my hold on Lauren's little hand. "Go on and play, baby doll. Mommy and I will be sitting on the bench. You've got ten minutes. We'll call you when it's time to go."

She let out a squeal of delight and ran to the slide, her golden curls bouncing on her shoulders. I stood there as she zipped up the steps and perched at the top of the slide. She glanced back at us, waved, and plummeted down the plastic tube. My heart plunged into my stomach. Sandy gently grabbed my hand and gave a small tug.

"Let's go sit on the bench," she said, guiding me away.

I sat on the edge of my seat with my eyes glued to Lauren. I swallowed, watching as kids of all ages swarmed the playscape. They ran up and down the stairs, sliding down poles, climbing up slides. Their little voices sang out their joy in shrieks of laughter that reached the heavens. And there was my little Lauren joining in.

She ran all over the playscape, climbing, sliding, and jumping with the best of them. Every time her little blonde head disappeared around the steps, my heart jumped into my throat, only to come crashing back to my chest when she reappeared. Each time, Sandy would put a reassuring hand on my leg.

"Lauren's going to be fine," she would tell me, waiting for me to relax.

As I sat there and watched her, I noticed something. My baby girl wasn't a baby anymore.

She interacted with the other kids. She laughed with them. She was making friends and having a good time. And she was doing it without me hovering over her. It was almost as if she didn't need me anymore.

My emotions were in turmoil as this realization hit. To see Lauren interact with the other kids like a little adult filled me with relief and joy. She was learning and honing social skills she would need throughout her life. But my heart also broke as one thread from the apron string snapped. We had taken a step that could never be reversed. It was almost too much to comprehend—or maybe just more than I wanted to comprehend.

As I sat on that bench, the fear began to fade until it was a small, hard ball in the pit of my stomach. I could relax a little and enjoy watching Lauren play. Little ones really are fun to watch. There were some cringe-worthy moments when she stumbled, but the worst was done by another child.

I watched in horror as a boy no older than two tumbled five feet to the woodchips below. I jumped up not only to help him, but to trumpet this as a reason why I needed to be by my little daughter's side. He shattered my case when he bounced up and took off, a peal of laughter streaming back to us horrified adults. I settled back in my place next to Sandy and waited for this torture to be over.

I glanced at my watch every five seconds or so, willing the ten minutes to fly rather than crawl. Finally the minute hand declared that ten minutes had passed.

"It's time, babe," I said to Sandy, and bounded from the bench without waiting for an answer.

"Come on, Lauren," I called out, "It's time to get going."

"Okay, Daddy," her little voice chimed from the other side of the playscape.

She flew around the slide, little arms pumping for all they were worth as she raced toward me. I put my arms out as she came closer and she flung up her hands. I grabbed her and spun her around.

"Stop, Daddy," she giggled, "I'm getting dizzy."

I planted a kiss on her rosy cheek and set her on the ground. She grabbed my hand as we started for the car.

Looking down at her, I was finally able to grasp how big she really was. It hit me then that I had to start giving her some freedoms. I had to let her grow so that she could be her own person. As much as it pained me, I know the time would come when she would be completely on her own. My heart still ached with one question, though: Why did the process have to start so early in her life?

But as we walked through the grass, I found myself praising God that He lets us let go of our kids slowly, a day at a time, rather than all at once. Today was just a small step in a lifelong process. I knew there were tough days ahead—it would be hard to find the balance of letting go and holding on. But with God's help, I knew I would be up to the task. ◆

> Your ears shall hear a word behind you, saying,
> "This is the way, walk in it,"
> Whenever you turn to the right hand
> Or whenever you turn to the left.
>
> ISAIAH 30:21

QUALITY TIME

One of the best ways to make your kids feel secure and confident as they head out into the world is to spend time with them. Quality time makes kids feel important and loved, and it's a good opportunity to instill values and lend direction. Plus, one-on-one time is a good platform for you to get to know your kids and offer wisdom and advice.

Make an effort to spend time with each of your kids this week. It doesn't matter what you do, as long as they have your undivided attention.

As a bonus, spending time with your kids makes good use of the time you have with them—and gives you the kind of memories that soothe the sting of letting go. ◆

THE BEST THING TO SPEND ON
YOUR CHILDREN IS YOUR TIME.

LOUISE HART

THE GREATEST GIFTS YOU CAN
GIVE YOUR CHILDREN ARE THE
ROOTS OF RESPONSIBILITY AND
THE WINGS OF INDEPENDENCE.

DENIS WAITLEY

ALWAYS THERE

JEANETTE LITTLETON

When I was growing up, few malls existed in Kansas City besides strip malls. But my family lived less than a mile from one of those few malls—a then-outdoor mall called the Antioch Shopping Center.

Saturday was designated as shopping day in our home, and many Saturdays, as the need arose, we would go to Antioch. Mom would visit Grant's, TG&Y, and the drugstore for thread, material, and other household items. My older brother would be off walking around the mall and doing the things guys do.

When I grew old enough to get a little taste of independence, Dad would sit on a cement bench in an outdoor foyer of the stores, and I would dash about. I'd climb down the crooked, chipped linoleum steps to the basement treasure trove of toys. I'd eye the merchandise, imagining what I would buy if I could save my allowance.

After I carefully perused the aisles of interest to me at TG&Y and the small pet center in the back of the basement, I'd go back up those slanted stairs and trot over to the old-fashioned candy counters, peering through the glass at all the penny candies spread out.

Once I'd taken inventory, I'd dash out the heavy glass door and over to dad. "Are you doing okay?" I'd ask solicitously. Dad would reassure me that he was fine. Then I'd run off again, returning between stores to make sure Dad was okay, and to make sure he was still there.

I never feared getting lost at the shopping center, or getting left behind—because Dad was always sitting on that cement bench waiting for me. Not once did he even step away for a few minutes, making me wait for him to return. No, as long as I was out and about, I could count on Dad to always be there.

Maybe that's part of what made me the independent person I am today—that early independence training.

And it still holds true. No matter where I roam or dash off to, I have learned as an adult that I can always count on Dad to be there. ◆

He has put his angels in charge
of you to watch over you wherever you go.

PSALM 91:11 NCV

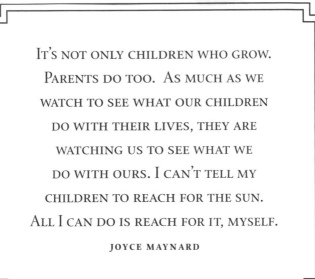

It's not only children who grow.
Parents do too. As much as we
watch to see what our children
do with their lives, they are
watching us to see what we
do with ours. I can't tell my
children to reach for the sun.
All I can do is reach for it, myself.

JOYCE MAYNARD

"For I know the plans I have for you,"
declares the Lord, "plans to prosper you and not
to harm you, plans to give you hope and a future."

JEREMIAH 29:11 NIV

God's Promises for Letting Go

Even to your old age and gray hairs I am he,
I am he who will sustain you. I have made you and
I will carry you; I will sustain you and I will rescue you.

ISAIAH 46:4 NIV

Trust in the LORD with all your heart, And lean not
on your own understanding; In all your ways
acknowledge Him, And He shall direct your paths.

PROVERBS 3:5–6

The children of Your servants will continue,
And their descendants will be established before You.

PSALM 102:28

Look at the new thing I am going to do. It is
already happening. Don't you see it? I will make
a road in the desert and rivers in the dry land.

ISAIAH 43:19 NCV

ACKNOWLEDGMENTS

"Always There" © Jeanette Littleton. Used by permission. All rights reserved.

"Come and Fish" © Sharon Hinck. Used by permission. All rights reserved.

"The Everlasting Arms" © Margaret Lang. Used by permission. All rights reserved.

"A Father's Call" © Lanita Bradley Boyd. Used by permission. All rights reserved.

"Free Walker" © Glenn A. Hascall. Used by permission. All rights reserved.

"If You're Gonna Quit, Don't Tell Daddy" © Max Davis. Used by permission. All rights reserved.

"Just Love Her" © Barbara M. Haller. Used by permission. All rights reserved.

"A Little Bit Better Than Yesterday" © Jeremy Moore. Used by permission. All rights reserved.

"Love Is Blind" © Michael T. Powers. Used by permission. All rights reserved.

"Lunch with Lenny" © Lanita Bradley Boyd. Used by permission. All rights reserved.

"The Nail" © Max Davis. Used by permission. All rights reserved.

"The New Father Fog" © Michael T. Powers. Used by permission. All rights reserved.

"The Rules of Engagement" © Jay Cookingham. Used by permission. All rights reserved.

"Starting Young" © Shane Werlinger. Used by permission. All rights reserved.

"Tuxedo Swimming" © Michael T. Powers. Used by permission. All rights reserved.

"A Very Lucky Man" © Nancy B. Gibbs. Used by permission. All rights reserved.

"Where There's a Will, There's a Way" © Renie Burghardt. Used by permission. All rights reserved.

"Words" © Sally Clark. Used by permission. All rights reserved.